The Trespa

Volume 2

Gilbert Parker

Alpha Editions

This edition published in 2024

ISBN : 9789362098368

Design and Setting By
Alpha Editions
www.alphaedis.com
Email - info@alphaedis.com

As per information held with us this book is in Public Domain.
This book is a reproduction of an important historical work. Alpha Editions uses the best technology to reproduce historical work in the same manner it was first published to preserve its original nature. Any marks or number seen are left intentionally to preserve its true form.

Contents

VOLUME 2. .... - 1 -
CHAPTER VI .... - 3 -
CHAPTER VII .... - 10 -
CHAPTER VIII .... - 20 -
CHAPTER IX .... - 27 -
CHAPTER X .... - 35 -
CHAPTER XI .... - 43 -

VOLUME 2.

CHAPTER VI

WHICH TELLS OF STRANGE ENCOUNTERS

A few hours afterwards Gaston sat on his horse, in a quiet corner of the grounds, while his uncle sketched him. After a time he said that Saracen would remain quiet no longer. His uncle held up the sketch. Gaston could scarcely believe that so strong and life-like a thing were possible in the time. It had force and imagination. He left his uncle with a nod, rode quietly through the park, into the village, and on to the moor. At the top he turned and looked down. The perfectness of the landscape struck him; it was as if the picture had all grown there—not a suburban villa, not a modern cottage, not one tall chimney of a manufactory, but just the sweet common life. The noises of the village were soothing, the soft smell of the woodland came over. He watched a cart go by idly, heavily clacking.

As he looked, it came to him: was his uncle right after all? Was he out of place here? He was not a part of this, though he had adapted himself and had learned many fine social ways. He knew that he lived not exactly as though born here and grown up with it all. But it was also true that he had a native sense of courtesy which people called distinguished. There was ever a kind of mannered deliberation in his bearing—a part of his dramatic temper, and because his father had taught him dignity where there were no social functions for its use. His manner had, therefore, a carefulness which in him was elegant artifice.

It could not be complained that he did not act after the fashion of gentle people when with them. But it was equally true that he did many things which the friends of his family could not and would not have done. For instance, none would have pitched a tent in the grounds, slept in it, read in it, and lived in it—when it did not rain. Probably no one of them would have, at individual expense, sent the wife of the village policeman to a hospital in London, to be cured—or to die—of cancer. None would have troubled to insist that a certain stagnant pool in the village be filled up. Nor would one have suddenly risen in court and have acted as counsel for a gipsy! At the same time, all were too well- bred to think that Gaston did this because the gipsy had a daughter with him, a girl of strong, wild beauty, with a look of superiority over her position.

He thought of all the circumstances now.

It was very many months ago. The man had been accused of stealing and assault, but the evidence was unconvincing to Gaston. The feeling in court was against the gipsy. Fearing a verdict against him, Gaston rose and cross-examined the witnesses, and so adroitly bewildered both them and the justices who sat with his grandfather on the case, that, at last, he secured the man's freedom. The girl was French, and knew English imperfectly. Gaston had her sworn, and made the most of her evidence. Then, learning that an assault had been made on the gipsy's van by some lads who worked at mills in a neighbouring town, he pushed for their arrest, and himself made up the loss to the gipsy.

It is possible that there was in the mind of the girl what some common people thought: that the thing was done for her favour; for she viewed it half-gratefully, half-frowningly, till, on the village green, Gaston asked her father what he wished to do—push on or remain to act against the lads.

The gipsy, angry as he was, wished to move on. Gaston lifted his hat to the girl and bade her good-bye. Then she saw that his motives had been wholly unselfish—even quixotic, as it appeared to her—silly, she would have called it, if silliness had not seemed unlikely in him. She had never met a man like him before. She ran her fingers through her golden- brown hair nervously, caught at a flying bit of old ribbon at her waist, and said in French:

"He is honest altogether, sir. He did not steal, and he was not there when it happened."

"I know that, my girl. That is why I did it."

She looked at him keenly. Her eyes ran up and down his figure, then met his curiously. Their looks swam for a moment. Something thrilled in them both. The girl took a step nearer.

"You are as much a Romany here as I am," she said, touching her bosom with a quick gesture. "You do not belong; you are too good for it. How do I know? I do not know; I feel. I will tell your fortune," she suddenly added, reaching for his hand. "I have only known three that I could do it with honestly and truly, and you are one. It is no lie. There is something in it. My mother had it; but it's all sham mostly." Then, under a tree on the green, he indifferent to village gossip, she took his hand and told him—not of his fortune alone. In half-coherent fashion she told him of the past—of his life in the North. She then spoke of his future. She told him of a woman, of another, and another still; of an accident at sea, and of a quarrel; then, with a low, wild laugh, she stopped, let go his hand, and would say no more. But her face was all flushed, and her eyes like burning beads. Her father stood near, listening. Now he took her by the arm.

"Here, Andree, that's enough," he said, with rough kindness; "it's no good for you or him."

He turned to Gaston, and said in English:

"She's sing'lar, like her mother afore her. But she's straight."

Gaston lit a cigar.

"Of course." He looked kindly at the girl. "You are a weird sort, Andree, and perhaps you are right that I'm a Romany too; but I don't know where it begins and where it ends. You are not English gipsies?" he added, to the father.

"I lived in England when I was young. Her mother was a Breton—not a Romany. We're on the way to France now. She wants to see where her mother was born. She's got the Breton lingo, and she knows some English; but she speaks French mostly."

"Well, well," rejoined Gaston, "take care of yourself, and good luck to you. Good-bye—good-bye, Andree." He put his hand in his pocket to give her some money, but changed his mind. Her eye stopped him. He shook hands with the man, then turned to her again. Her eyes were on him—hot, shining. He felt his blood throb, but he returned the look with good-natured nonchalance, shook her hand, raised his hat, and walked away, thinking what a fine, handsome creature she was. Presently he said: "Poor girl, she'll look at some fellow like that one day, with tragedy the end thereof!"

He then fell to wondering about her almost uncanny divination. He knew that all his life he himself had had strange memories, as well as certain peculiar powers which had put the honest phenomena and the trickery of the Medicine Men in the shade. He had influenced people by the sheer force of presence. As he walked on, he came to a group of trees in the middle of the common. He paused for a moment, and looked back. The gipsy's van was moving away, and in the doorway stood the girl, her hand over her eyes, looking towards him. He could see the raw colour of her scarf. "She'll make wild trouble," he said to himself.

As Gaston thought of this event, he moved his horse slowly towards a combe, and looked out over a noble expanse—valley, field, stream, and church-spire. As he gazed, he saw seated at some distance a girl reading. Not far from her were two boys climbing up and down the combe. He watched them. Presently he saw one boy creep along a shelf of rock where the combe broke into a quarry, let himself drop upon another shelf below, and then perch upon an overhanging ledge. He presently saw that the lad was now afraid to return. He heard the other lad cry out, saw the girl start up, and run forward, look over the edge of the combe, and then make as if to go down. He set his horse to the gallop, and called out. The girl saw him, and paused. In two minutes he was off his horse and beside her.

It was Alice Wingfield. She had brought out three boys, who had come with her from London, where she had spent most of the year nursing their sick mother, her relative.

"I'll have him up in a minute," he said, as he led Saracen to a sapling near. "Don't go near the horse."

He swung himself down from ledge to ledge, and soon was beside the boy. In another moment he had the youngster on his back, came slowly up, and the adventurer was safe.

"Silly Walter," the girl said, "to frighten yourself and give Mr. Belward trouble."

"I didn't think I'd be afraid," protested the lad; "but when I looked over the ledge my head went round, and I felt sick—like with the channel."

Gaston had seen Alice Wingfield several times at church and in the village, and once when, with Lady Belward, he had returned the archdeacon's call; but she had been away most of the time since his arrival. She had impressed him as a gentle, wise, elderly little creature, who appeared to live for others, and chiefly for her grandfather. She was not unusually pretty, nor yet young,—quite as old as himself,—and yet he wondered what it was that made her so interesting. He decided that it was the honesty of her nature, her beautiful thoroughness; and then he thought little more about her. But now he dropped into quiet, natural talk with her, as if they had known each other for years. But most women found that they dropped quickly into easy talk with him. That was because he had not learned the small gossip which varies little with a thousand people in the same circumstances. But he had a naive fresh sense, everything interested him, and he said what he thought with taste and tact, sometimes with wit, and always in that cheerful contemplative mood which influences women. Some of his sayings were so startling and heretical that they had gone the rounds, and certain crisp words out of the argot of the North were used by women who wished to be chic and amusing.

Not quite certain why he stayed, but talking on reflectively, Gaston at last said:

"You will be coming to us to-night, of course? We are having a barbecue of some kind."

"Yes, I hope so; though my grandfather does not much care to have me go."

"I suppose it is dull for him."

"I am not sure it is that."

"No? What then?"

She shook her head.

"The affair is in your honour, Mr. Belward, isn't it?"

"Does that answer my question?" he asked genially.

She blushed.

"No, no, no! That is not what I meant."

"I was unfair. Yes, I believe the matter does take that colour; though why, I don't know."

She looked at him with simple earnestness.

"You ought to be proud of it; and you ought to be glad of such a high position where you can do so much good, if you will."

He smiled, and ran his hand down his horse's leg musingly before he replied:

"I've not thought much of doing good, I tell you frankly. I wasn't brought up to think about it; I don't know that I ever did any good in my life. I supposed it was only missionaries and women who did that sort of thing."

"But you wrong yourself. You have done good in this village. Why, we all have talked of it; and though it wasn't done in the usual way—rather irregularly—still it was doing good."

He looked down at her astonished.

"Well, here's a pretty libel! Doing good 'irregularly'? Why, where have I done good at all?"

She ran over the names of several sick people in the village whose bills he had paid, the personal help and interest he had given to many, and, last of all, she mentioned the case of the village postmaster.

Since Gaston had come, postmasters had been changed. The little pale-faced man who had first held the position disappeared one night, and in another twenty-four hours a new one was in his place. Many stories had gone about. It was rumoured that the little man was short in his accounts, and had been got out of the way by Gaston Belward. Archdeacon Varcoe knew the truth, and had said that Gaston's sin was not unpardonable, in spite of a few squires and their dames who declared it was shocking that a man should have such loose ideas, that no good could come to the county from it, and that he would put nonsense into the heads of the common people. Alice Wingfield was now to hear Gaston's view of the matter.

"So that's it, eh? Live and let live is doing good? In that case it is easy to be a saint. What else could a man do? You say that I am generous—How? What have I spent out of my income on these little things? My income—how did I get it? I didn't earn it; neither did my father. Not a stroke have I done for it. I sit high and dry there in the Court, they sit low there in the village; and you know how they live. Well, I give away a little money which these people and their fathers earned for my father and me; and for that you say I am doing good, and some other people say I am doing harm—'dangerous charity,' and all that! I say that the little I have done is what is always done where man is most primitive, by people who never heard 'doing good' preached."

"We must have names for things, you know," she said.

"I suppose so, where morality and humanity have to be taught as Christian duty, and not as common manhood."

"Tell me," she presently said, "about Sproule, the postmaster."

"Oh, that? Well, I will. The first time I entered the post-office I saw there was something on the man's mind. A youth of twenty-three oughtn't to look as he did—married only a year or two also, with a pretty wife and child. I used to talk to them a good deal, and one day I said to him: 'You look seedy; what's the matter?' He flushed, and got nervous. I made up my mind it was money. If I had been here longer, I should have taken him aside and talked to him like a father. As it was, things slid along. I was up in town, and here and there. One evening as I came back from town I saw a nasty-looking Jew arrive. The little postmaster met him, and they went away together. He was in the scoundrel's hands; had been betting, and had borrowed first from the Jew, then from the Government. The next evening I was just starting down to have a talk with him, when an official came to my grandfather to swear out a warrant. I lost no time; got my horse and trap, went down to the office, gave the boy three minutes to tell me the truth, and then I sent him away. I fixed it up with the authorities, and the wife and child follow the youth to America next week. That's all."

"He deserved to get free, then?"

"He deserved to be punished, but not as he would have been. There wasn't really a vicious spot in the man. And the wife and child—what was a little justice to the possible happiness of those three? Discretion is a part of justice, and I used it, as it is used every day in business and judicial life, only we don't see it. When it gets public, why, some one gets blamed. In this case I was the target; but I don't mind in the least—not in the least. . . . Do you think me very startling or lawless?"

"Never lawless; but one could not be quite sure what you would do in any particular case." She looked up at him admiringly.

They had not noticed the approach of Archdeacon Varcoe till he was very near them. His face was troubled. He had seen how earnest was their conversation, and for some reason it made him uneasy. The girl saw him first, and ran to meet him. He saw her bright delighted look, and he sighed involuntarily. "Something has worried you," she said caressingly. Then she told him of the accident, and they all turned and went back towards the Court, Gaston walking his horse. Near the church they met Sir William and Lady Belward. There were salutations, and presently Gaston slowly followed his grandfather and grandmother into the courtyard.

Sir William, looking back, said to his wife: "Do you think that Gaston should be told?"

"No, no, there is no danger. Gaston, my dear, shall marry Delia Gasgoyne."

"Shall marry? wherefore 'shall'? Really, I do not see."

"She likes him, she is quite what we would have her, and he is interested in her. My dear, I have seen—I have watched for a year."

He put his hand on hers.

"My wife, you are a goodly prophet."

When Archdeacon Varcoe entered his study on returning, he sat down in a chair, and brooded long. "She must be told," he said at last, aloud. "Yes, yes, at once. God help us both!"

CHAPTER VII

WHEREIN THE SEAL OF HIS HERITAGE IS SET

"Sophie, when you talk with the man, remember that you are near fifty, and faded. Don't be sentimental." So said Mrs. Gasgoyne to Lady Dargan, as they saw Gaston coming down the ballroom with Captain Maudsley.

"Reine, you try one's patience. People would say you were not quite disinterested."

"You mean Delia! Now, listen. I haven't any wish but that Gaston Belward shall see Delia very seldom indeed. He will inherit the property no doubt, and Sir William told me that he had settled a decent fortune on him; but for Delia—no—no—no. Strange, isn't it, when Lady Harriet over there aches for him, Indian blood and all? And why? Because this is a good property, and the fellow is distinguished and romantic-looking: but he is impossible—perfectly impossible. Every line of his face says shipwreck."

"You are not usually so prophetic."

"Of course. But I am prophetic now, for Delia is more than interested, silly chuck! Did you ever read the story of the other Gaston—Sir Gaston—whom this one resembles? No? Well, you will find it thinly disguised in The Knight of Five Joys. He was killed at Naseby, my dear; killed, not by the enemy, but by a page in Rupert's cavalry. The page was a woman! It's in this one too. Indian and French blood is a sad tincture. He is not wicked at heart, not at all; but he will do mad things yet, my dear. For he'll tire of all this, and then—half-mourning for some one!"

Gaston enjoyed talking with Mrs. Gasgoyne as to no one else. Other women often flattered him, she never did. Frankly, crisply, she told him strange truths, and, without mercy, crumbled his wrong opinions. He had a sense of humour, and he enjoyed her keen chastening raillery. Besides, her talk was always an education in the fine lights and shadows of this social life. He came to her now with a smile, greeted her heartily, and then turned to Lady Dargan. Captain Maudsley carried off Mrs. Gasgoyne, and the two were left together—the second time since the evening of Gaston's arrival, so many months before. Lady Dargan had been abroad, and was just returned.

They talked a little on unimportant things, and presently Lady Dargan said:

"Pardon my asking, but will you tell me why you wore a red ribbon in your button-hole the first night you came?"

He smiled, and then looked at her a little curiously. "My luggage had not come, and I wore an old suit of my father's."

Lady Dargan sighed deeply.

"The last night he was in England he wore that coat at dinner," she murmured.

"Pardon me, Lady Dargan—you put that ribbon there?"

"Yes."

Her eyes were on him with a candid interest and regard.

"I suppose," he went on, "that his going was abrupt to you?"

"Very—very!" she answered.

She longed to ask if his father ever mentioned her name, but she dared not. Besides, as she said to herself, to what good now? But she asked him to tell her something about his father. He did so quietly, picking out main incidents, and setting them forth, as he had the ability, with quiet dramatic strength. He had just finished when Delia Gasgoyne came up with Lord Dargan.

Presently Lord Dargan asked Gaston if he would bring Lady Dargan to the other end of the room, where Miss Gasgoyne was to join her mother. As they went, Lady Dargan said a little breathlessly:

"Will you do something for me?"

"I would do much for you," was his reply, for he understood!

"If ever you need a friend, if ever you are in trouble, will you let me know? I wish to take an interest in you. Promise me."

'I cannot promise, Lady Dargan," he answered, "for such trouble as I have had before I have had to bear alone, and the habit is fixed, I fear. Still, I am grateful to you just the same, and I shall never forget it. But will you tell me why people regard me from so tragical a stand-point?"

"Do they?"

"Well, there's yourself, and there's Mrs. Gasgoyne, and there's my uncle Ian."

"Perhaps we think you may have trouble because of your uncle Ian."

Gaston shook his head enigmatically, and then said ironically:

"As they would put it in the North, Lady Dargan, he'll cut no figure in that matter. I remember for two."

"That is right—that is right. Always think that Ian Belward is bad—bad at heart. He is as fascinating as—"

"As the Snake?"

"—as the Snake, and as cruel! It is the cruelty of wicked selfishness. Somehow, I forget that I am talking to his nephew. But we all know Ian Belward—at least, all women do."

"And at least one man does," he answered gravely. The next minute Gaston walked down the room with Delia Gasgoyne on his arm. The girl delicately showed her preference, and he was aware of it. It pleased him—pleased his unconscious egoism. The early part of his life had been spent among Indian women, half-breeds, and a few dull French or English folk, whose chief charm was their interest in that wild, free life, now so distant. He had met Delia many times since his coming; and there was that in her manner—a fine high-bred quality, a sweet speaking reserve—which interested him. He saw her as the best product of this convention.

She was no mere sentimental girl, for she had known at least six seasons, and had refused at least six lovers. She had a proud mind, not wide, suited to her position. Most men had flattered her, had yielded to her; this man, either with art or instinctively, mastered her, secured her interest by his personality. Every woman worth the having, down in her heart, loves to be mastered: it gives her a sense of security, and she likes to lean; for, strong as she may be at times, she is often singularly weak. She knew that her mother deprecated "that Belward enigma," but this only sent her on the dangerous way.

To-night she questioned him about his life, and how he should spend the summer. Idling in France, he said. And she? She was not sure; but she thought that she also would be idling about France in her father's yacht. So they might happen to meet. Meanwhile? Well, meanwhile, there were people coming to stay at Peppingham, their home. August would see that over. Then freedom.

Was it freedom, to get away from all this—from England and rule and measure? No, she did not mean quite that. She loved the life with all its rules; she could not live without it. She had been brought up to expect and to do certain things. She liked her comforts, her luxuries, many pretty things about her, and days without friction. To travel? Yes, with all modern comforts, no long stages, a really good maid, and some fresh interesting books.

What kind of books? Well, Walter Pater's essays; "The Light of Asia"; a novel of that wicked man Thomas Hardy; and something light—"The Innocents Abroad"—with, possibly, a struggle through De Musset, to keep up her French.

It did not seem exciting to Gaston, but it did sound honest, and it was in the picture. He much preferred Meredith, and Swinburne, and Dumas, and Hugo; but with her he did also like the whimsical Mark Twain.

He thought of suggestions that Lady Belward had often thrown out; of those many talks with Sir William, excellent friends as they were, in which the baronet hinted at the security he would feel if there was a second family of Belwards. What if he—? He smiled strangely, and shrank.

Marriage? There was the touchstone.

After the dance, when he was taking her to her mother, he saw a pale intense face looking out to him from a row of others. He smiled, and the smile that came in return was unlike any he had ever seen Alice Wingfield wear. He was puzzled. It flashed to him strange pathos, affection, and entreaty. He took Delia Gasgoyne to her mother, talked to Lady Belward a little, and then went quietly back to where he had seen Alice. She was gone. Just then some people from town came to speak to him, and he was detained. When he was free he searched, but she was nowhere to be found. He went to Lady Belward. Yes, Miss Wingfield had gone. Lady Belward looked at Gaston anxiously, and asked him why he was curious. "Because she's a lonely-looking little maid," he said, "and I wanted to be kind to her. She didn't seem happy a while ago."

Lady Belward was reassured.

'Yes, she is a sweet creature, Gaston," she said, and added: "You are a good boy to-night, a very good host indeed. It is worth the doing," she went on, looking out on the guests proudly. "I did not think I should ever come to it again with any heart, but I do it for you gladly. Now, away to your duty," she added, tapping his breast affectionately with her fan, "and when everything is done, come and take me to my room."

Ian Belward passed Gaston as he went. He had seen the affectionate passages.

"'For a good boy!' 'God bless our Home!'" he said, ironically.

Gaston saw the mark of his hand on his uncle's chin, and he forbore ironical reply.

"The home is worth the blessing," he rejoined quietly, and passed on.

Three hours later the guests had all gone, and Lady Belward, leaning on her grandson's arm, went to her boudoir, while Ian and his father sought the library. Ian was going next morning. The conference was not likely to be cheerful.

Inside her boudoir, Lady Belward sank into a large chair, and let her head fall back and her eyes close. She motioned Gaston to a seat. Taking one near, he waited. After a time she opened her eyes and drew herself up.

"My dear," she said, "I wish to talk with you."

"I shall be very glad; but isn't it late? and aren't you tired, grandmother?"

"I shall sleep better after," she responded, gently. She then began to review the past; her own long unhappiness, Robert's silence, her uncertainty as to his fate, and the after hopelessness, made greater by Ian's conduct. In low, kind words she spoke of his coming and the renewal of her hopes, coupled with fear also that he might not fit in with his new life, and—she could say it now—do something unbearable. Well, he had done nothing unworthy of their name; had acted, on the whole, sensibly; and she had not been greatly surprised at certain little oddnesses, such as the tent in the grounds, an impossible deer-hunt, and some unusual village charities and innovations on the estate. Nor did she object to Brillon, though he had sometimes thrown servants'-hall into disorder, and had caused the stablemen and the footmen to fight. His ear-rings and hair were startling, but they were not important. Gaston had been admired by the hunting-field—of which they were glad, for it was a test of popularity. She saw that most people liked him. Lord Dunfolly and Admiral Highburn were enthusiastic. For her own part, she was proud and grateful. She could enjoy every grain of comfort he gave them; and she was thankful to make up to Robert's son what Robert himself had lost—poor boy—poor boy!

Her feelings were deep, strong, and sincere. Her grandson had come, strong, individual, considerate, and had moved the tender courses of her nature. At this moment Gaston had his first deep feeling of responsibility.

"My dear," she said at last, "people in our position have important duties. Here is a large estate. Am I not clear? You will never be quite part of this life till you bring a wife here. That will give you a sense of responsibility. You will wake up to many things then. Will you not marry? There is Delia Gasgoyne. Your grandfather and I would be so glad. She is worthy in every way, and she likes you. She is a good girl. She has never frittered her heart away; and she would make you proud of her."

She reached out an anxious hand, and touched his shoulder. His eyes were playing with the pattern of the carpet; but he slowly raised them to hers, and looked for a moment without speaking. Suddenly, in spite of himself, he laughed—laughed outright, but not loudly.

Marriage? Yes, here was the touchstone. Marry a girl whose family had been notable for hundreds of years? For the moment he did not remember his own family. This was one of the times when he was only conscious that he had savage blood, together with a strain of New World French, and that his life had mostly been a range of adventure and common toil. This new position was his right, but there were times when it seemed to him that he was an impostor; others, when he felt himself master of it all, when he even had a sense of superiority—why he could not tell; but life in this old land of tradition and history had not its due picturesqueness. With his grandmother's proposal there shot up in him the thought that for him this was absurd. He to pace the world beside this fine queenly creature—Delia Gasgoyne—carrying on the traditions of the Belwards! Was it, was it possible?

"Pardon me," he said at last gently, as he saw Lady Belward shrink and then look curiously at him, "something struck me, and I couldn't help it."

"Was what I said at all ludicrous?"

"Of course not; you said what was natural for you to say, and I thought what was natural for me to think, at first blush."

"There is something wrong," she urged fearfully. "Is there any reason why you cannot marry? Gaston,"—she trembled towards him,—"you have not deceived us—you are not married?"

"My wife is dead, as I told you," he answered gravely, musingly.

"Tell me: there is no woman who has a claim on you?"

"None that I know of—not one. My follies have not run that way."

"Thank God! Then there is no reason why you should not marry. Oh, when I look at you I am proud, I am glad that I live! You bring my youth, my son back; and I long for a time when I may clasp your child in my arms, and know that Robert's heritage will go on and on, and that there will be made up to him, somehow, all that he lost. Listen: I am an old, crippled, suffering woman; I shall soon have done with all this coming and going, and I speak to you out of the wisdom of sorrow. Had Robert married, all would have gone well. He did not: he got into trouble, then came Ian's hand in it all; and you know the end. I fear for you, I do indeed. You will have sore temptations. Marry—marry soon, and make us happy."

He was quiet enough now. He had seen the grotesque image, now he was facing the thing behind it. "Would it please you so very much?" he said, resting a hand gently on hers.

"I wish to see a child of yours in my arms, dear."

"And the woman you have chosen is Delia Gasgoyne?"

"The choice is for you; but you seem to like each other, and we care for her."

He sat thinking for a time, then he got up, and said slowly:

"It shall be so, if Miss Gasgoyne will have me. And I hope it may turn out as you wish."

Then he stooped and kissed her on the cheek. The proud woman, who had unbent little in her lifetime, whose eyes had looked out so coldly on the world, who felt for her son Ian an almost impossible aversion, drew down his head and kissed it.

"Indian and all?" he asked, with a quaint bitterness.

"Everything, my dear," she answered. "God bless you! Good-night."

A few moments after, Gaston went to the library. He heard the voices of Sir William and his uncle. He knocked and entered. Ian, with exaggerated courtesy, rose. Gaston, with easy coolness, begged him to sit, lit a cigar, and himself sat.

"My father has been feeding me with raw truths, Cadet," said his uncle; "and I've been eating them unseasoned. We have not been, nor are likely to be, a happy family, unless in your saturnian reign we learn to say, pax vobiscum—do you know Latin? For I'm told the money-bags and the stately pile are for you. You are to beget children before the Lord, and sit in the seat of Justice: 'tis for me to confer honour on you all by my genius!"

Gaston sat very still, and, when the speech was ended, said tentatively:

"Why rob yourself?"

"In honouring you all?"

"No, sir; in not yourself having 'a saturnian reign'."

"You are generous."

"No: I came here to ask for a home, for what was mine through my father. I ask, and want, nothing more—not even to beget children before the Lord!"

"How mellow the tongue! Well, Cadet, I am not going to quarrel. Here we are with my father. See, I am willing to be friends. But you mustn't expect that I will not chasten your proud spirit now and then. That you need it, this morning bears witness."

Sir William glanced from one to the other curiously. He was cold and calm, and looked worn. He had had a trying half-hour with his son, and it had told on him.

Gaston at once said to his grandfather: "Of this morning, sir, I will tell you. I—"

Ian interrupted him.

"No, no; that is between us. Let us not worry my father."

Sir William smiled ironically.

"Your solicitude is refreshing, Ian."

"Late fruit is the sweetest, sir."

Presently Sir William asked Gaston the result of the talk with Lady Belward. Gaston frankly said that he was ready to do as they wished. Sir William then said they had chosen this time because Ian was there, and it was better to have all open and understood.

Ian laughed.

"Taming the barbarian! How seriously you all take it. I am the jester for the King. In the days of the flood I'll bring the olive leaf. You are all in the wash of sentiment: you'll come to the wicked uncle one day for common-sense. But, never mind, Cadet; we are to be friends. Yes, really. I do not fear for my heritage, and you'll need a helping hand one of these days. Besides, you are an interesting fellow. So, if you will put up with my acid tongue, there's no reason why we shouldn't hit it off."

To Sir William's great astonishment, Ian held out his hand with a genial smile, which was tolerably honest, for his indulgent nature was as capable of great geniality as incapable of high moral conceptions. Then, he had before his eye, "Monmouth" and "The King of Ys."

Gaston took his hand, and said: "I have no wish to be an enemy."

Sir William rose, looking at them both. He could not understand Ian's attitude, and he distrusted. Yet peace was better than war. Ian's truce was also based on a belief that Gaston would make skittles of things. A little while afterwards Gaston sat in his room, turning over events in his mind. Time and again his thoughts returned to the one thing— marriage. That marriage with his Esquimaux wife had been in one sense none at all, for the end was sure from the beginning. It was in keeping with his youth, the circumstances, the life, it had no responsibilities. But this? To become an integral part of the life—the English country gentleman; to be reduced, diluted, to the needs of the convention, and no more? Let him think of the details:—a justice of the peace: to sit on a board of directors; to be, perhaps, Master of the Hounds; to unite with the Bishop in restoring the cathedral; to make an address at the annual flower show. His wife to open bazaars, give tennis-parties, and be patron to the clergy; himself at last, no doubt, to go into Parliament: to feel the petty, or serious, responsibilities of a husband and a landlord. Monotony, extreme decorum, civility to the world; endless politeness to his wife; with boys at Eton and girls somewhere else; and the kind of man he must be to do his duty in all and to all!

It seemed impossible. He rose and paced the floor. Never till this moment had the full picture of his new life come close. He felt stifled. He put on a cap, and, descending the stairs, went out into the court-yard and walked about, the cool air refreshing him. Gradually there settled upon him a stoic acceptance of the conditions. But would it last?

He stood still and looked at the pile of buildings before him; then he turned towards the little church close by, whose spire and roof could be seen above the wall. He waved his hand, as when within it on the day of his coming, and said with irony:

"Now for the marriage-linen, Sir Gaston!"

He heard a low knocking at the gate. He listened. Yes, there was no mistake. He went to it, and asked quietly:

"Who is there?"

There was no reply. Still the knocking went on. He quietly opened the gate, and threw it back. A figure in white stepped through and slowly passed him. It was Alice Wingfield. He spoke to her. She did not answer. He went close to her and saw that she was asleep!

She was making for the entrance door. He took her hand gently, and led her into a side door, and on into the ballroom. She moved towards a window through which the moonlight streamed, and sat on a cushioned bench beneath it. It was the spot where he had seen her at the dance. She leaned forward, looking into space, as she did at him then. He moved and got in her line of vision.

The picture was weird. She wore a soft white chamber-gown, her hair hung loose on her shoulders, her pale face cowled it in. The look was inexpressibly sad. Over her fell dim, coloured lights from the stained- glass windows; and shadowy ancestors looked silently down from the armour-hung walls.

To Gaston, collected as he was, it gave an ominous feeling. Why did she come here even in her sleep? What did that look mean? He gazed intently into her eyes.

All at once her voice came low and broken, and a sob followed the words:

"Gaston, my brother, my brother!"

He stood for a moment stunned, gazing helplessly at her passive figure.

"Gaston, my brother!" he repeated to himself. Then the painful matter dawned upon him. This girl, the granddaughter of the rector of the parish, was his father's daughter—his own sister. He had a sudden spring of new affection—unfelt for those other relations, his by the rights of the law and the gospel. The pathos of the thing caught him in the throat—for her how pitiful, how unhappy! He was sure that, somehow, she had only come to know of it since the afternoon. Then there had been so different a look in her face!

One thing was clear: he had no right to this secret, and it must be for now as if it had never been. He came to her, and took her hand. She rose. He led her from the room, out into the court-yard, and from there through the gate into the road.

All was still. They passed over to the rectory. Just inside the gate, Gaston saw a figure issue from the house, and come quickly towards them. It was the rector, excited, anxious.

Gaston motioned silence, and pointed to her. Then he briefly whispered how she had come. The clergyman said that he had felt uneasy about her, had gone to her room, and was just issuing in search of her. Gaston resigned her, softly advised not waking her, and bade the clergyman good- night.

But presently he turned, touched the arm of the old man, and said meaningly:

"I know."

The rector's voice shook as he replied: "You have not spoken to her?'

"No."

"You will not speak of it?"

"No."

"Unless I should die, and she should wish it?"

"Always as she wishes."

They parted, and Gaston returned to the Court.

CHAPTER VIII

HE ANSWERS AN AWKWARD QUESTION

The next morning Brillon brought a note from Ian Belward, which said that he was starting, and asked Gaston to be sure and come to Paris. The note was carelessly friendly. After reading it, he lay thinking. Presently he chanced to see Jacques look intently at him.

"Well, Brillon, what is it?" he asked genially. Jacques had come on better than Gaston had hoped for, but the light play of his nature was gone—he was grave, almost melancholy; and, in his way, as notable as his master. Their life in London had changed him much. A valet in St. James's Street was not a hunting comrade on the Coppermine River. Often when Jacques was left alone he stood at the window looking out on the gay traffic, scarcely stirring; his eyes slow, brooding. Occasionally, standing so, he would make the sacred gesture. One who heard him swear now and then, in a calm, deliberate way,— at the cook and the porter,— would have thought the matters in strange contrast. But his religion was a central habit, followed as mechanically as his appetite or the folding of his master's clothes. Besides, like most woodsmen, he was superstitious. Gaston was kind with him, keeping, however, a firm hand till his manner had become informed by the new duties. Jacques's greatest pleasure was his early morning visits to the stables. Here were Saracen and Jim the broncho-sleek, savage, playful. But he touched the highest point of his London experience when they rode in the Park.

In this Gaston remained singular. He rode always with Jacques. Perhaps he wished to preserve one possible relic of the old life, perhaps he liked this touch of drama; or both. It created notice, criticism, but he was superior to that. Time and again people asked him to ride, but he always pleaded another engagement. He would then be seen with Jacques plus Jacques's earrings and the wonderful hair, riding grandly in the Row. Jacques's eyes sparkled and a snatch of song came to his lips at these times.

No figures in the Park were so striking. There was nothing bizarre, but Gaston had a distinguished look, and women who had felt his hand at their waists in the dance the night before, now knew him, somehow, at a grave distance. Though Gaston did not say it to himself, these were the hours when he really was with the old life—lived it again—prairie, savannah, ice-plain, alkali desert. When, dismounting, the horses were taken and they went up the stairs, Gaston would softly lay his whip across Jacques's shoulders without speaking. This was their only ritual of camaraderie, and neglect of it would have fretted the half-breed. Never had man such a servant. No matter at what hour Gaston returned, he found Jacques waiting; and when he woke he found him ready, as now, on this morning, after a strange night.

"What is it, Jacques?" he repeated.

The old name! Jacques shivered a little with pleasure. Presently he broke out with:

"Monsieur, when do we go back?"

"Go back where?"

"To the North, monsieur."

"What's in your noddle now, Brillon?"

The impatient return to "Brillon" cut Jacques like a whip.

"Monsieur," he suddenly said, his face glowing, his hands opening nervously, "we have eat, we have drunk, we have had the dance and the great music here: is it enough? Sometimes as you sleep you call out, and you toss to the strokes of the tower-clock. When we lie on the Plains of Yath from sunset to sunrise, you never stir then. You remember when we sleep on the ledge of the Voshti mountain—so narrow that we were tied together? Well, we were as babes in blankets. In the Prairie of the Ten Stars your fingers were on the trigger firm as a bolt; here I have watch them shake with the coffee-cup. Monsieur, you have seen: is it enough? You have lived here: is it like the old lodge and the long trail?"

Gaston sat up in bed, looked in the mirror opposite, ran his fingers through his hair, regarded his hands, turning them over, and then, with sharp impatience, said:

"Go to hell!"

The little man's face flushed to his hair; he sucked in the air with a gasp. Without a word, he went to the dressing-table, poured out the shaving-water, threw a towel over his arm, and turned to come to the bed; but, all at once, he sidled back, put down the water, and furtively drew a sleeve across his eyes.

Gaston saw, and something suddenly burned in him. He dropped his eyes, slid out of bed, into his dressing-gown, and sat down.

Jacques made ready. He was not prepared to have Gaston catch him by the shoulders with a nervous grip, search his eyes, and say:

"You damned little fool, I'm not worth it!" Jacques's face shone.

"Every great man has his fool—alors!" was the happy reply.

"Jacques," Gaston presently said, "what's on your mind?"

'I saw—last night, monsieur," he said.

"You saw what?"

"I saw you in the court-yard with the lady." Gaston was now very grave.

"Did you recognise her?"

"No: she moved all as a spirit."

"Jacques, that matter is between you and me. I'm going to tell you, though, two things; and—where's your string of beads?"

Jacques drew out his rosary.

"That's all right. Mum as Manitou! She was asleep; she is my sister. And that is all, till there's need for you to know more."

In this new confidence Jacques was content. The life was a gilded mess, but he could endure it now. Three days passed. During that time Gaston was up to town twice; lunched at Lady Dargan's, and dined at Lord Dunfolly's. For his grandfather, who was indisposed, he was induced to preside at a political meeting in the interest of a wealthy local brewer, who confidently expected the seat, and, through gifts to the party, a knighthood. Before the meeting, in the gush of—as he put it "kindred aims," he laid a finger familiarly in Gaston's button-hole. Jacques, who was present, smiled, for he knew every change in his master's face, and he saw a glitter in his eye. He remembered when they two were in trouble with a gang of river-drivers, and one did this same thing rudely: how Gaston looked down, and said, with a devilish softness: "Take it away." And immediately after the man did so.

Mr. Sylvester Gregory Babbs, in a similar position, heard a voice say down at him, with a curious obliqueness:

"If you please!"

The keenest edge of it was lost on the flaring brewer, but his fingers dropped, and he twisted his heavy watchchain uneasily. The meeting began. Gaston in a few formal words, unconventional in idea, introduced Mr. Babbs as "a gentleman whose name was a household word in the county, who would carry into Parliament the civic responsibility shown in his private life, who would render his party a support likely to fulfil its purpose."

When he sat down, Captain Maudsley said: "That's a trifle vague, Belward."

"How can one treat him with importance?"

"He's the sort that makes a noise one way or another."

"Yes. Obituary: 'At his residence in Babbslow Square, yesterday, Sir S. G. Babbs, M. P., member of the London County Council. Sir S. G. Babbs, it will be remembered, gave L100,000 to build a home for the propagation of Vice, and—'"

"That's droll!"

"Why not Vice? 'Twould be just the same in his mind. He doesn't give from a sense of moral duty. Not he; he's a bungowawen!"

"What is that?"

"That's Indian. You buy a lot of Indian or halfbreed loafers with beaver-skins and rum, go to the Mount of the Burning Arrows, and these fellows dance round you and call you one of the lost race, the Mighty Men of the Kimash Hills. And they'll do that while the rum lasts. Meanwhile you get to think yourself a devil of a swell—you and the gods! . . . And now we had better listen to this bungowawen, hadn't we?"

The room was full, and on the platform were gentlemen come to support Sir William Belward. They were interested to see how Gaston would carry it off.

Mr. Babbs's speech was like a thousand others by the same kind of man. More speeches—some opposing—followed, and at last came the chairman to close the meeting. He addressed himself chiefly to a bunch of farmers, artisans, and labouring-men near. After some good-natured raillery at political meetings in general, the bigotry of party, the difficulty in getting the wheat from the chaff, and some incisive thrusts at those who promised the moon and gave a green cheese, who spent their time in berating their opponents, he said:

'There's a game that sailors play on board ship—men-o'-war and sailing-ships mostly. I never could quite understand it, nor could any officers ever tell me—the fo'castle for the men and the quarter-deck for the officers, and what's English to one is Greek to the other. Well, this was all I could see in the game. They sat about, sometimes talking, sometimes not. All at once a chap would rise and say, 'Allow me to speak, me noble lord,' and follow this by hitting some one of the party wherever the blow got in easiest—on the head, anywhere! [Laughter.] Then he would sit down seriously, and someone else spoke to his noble lordship. Nobody got angry at the knocks, and Heaven only knows what it was all about. That is much the way with politics, when it is played fair. But here is what I want particularly to say: We are not all born the same, nor can we live the same. One man is born a brute, and another a good sort; one a liar, and one an honest man; one has brains, and the other hasn't. Now, I've lived where, as they say, one man is as good as another. But he isn't, there or here. A weak man can't run with a strong. We have heard to-night a lot of talk for something and against something. It is over. Are you sure you have got what was meant clear in your mind? [Laughter, and 'Blowed if we'ave!'] Very well; do not worry about that. We have been playing a game of 'Allow me to speak, me noble lord!' And who is going to help you to get the most out of your country and your life isn't easy to know. But we can get hold of a few clear ideas, and measure things against them. I know and have talked with a good many of you here ['That's so! That's so!'], and you know my ideas pretty well—that they are honest at least, and that I have seen the countries where freedom is 'on the job,' as they say. Now, don't put your faith in men and in a party that cry, 'We will make all things new,' to the tune of, 'We are a band of brothers.' Trust in one that says, 'You cannot undo the centuries. Take off the roof, remove a wall, let in the air, throw out a wing, but leave the old foundations.' And that is the real difference between the other party and mine; and these political games of ours come to that chiefly."

Presently he called for the hands of the meeting. They were given for Mr. Babbs.

Suddenly a man's strong, arid voice came from the crowd:

"'Allow me to speak, me noble lord!' [Great laughter. Then a pause.] Where's my old chum, Jock Lawson?"

The audience stilled. Gaston's face went grave. He replied, in a firm, clear voice.

"In Heaven, my man. You'll never see him more." There was silence for a moment, a murmur, then a faint burst of applause. Presently John Cawley, the landlord of "The Whisk o' Barley," made towards Gaston. Gaston greeted him, and inquired after his wife. He was told that she was very ill, and had sent her husband to beg Gaston to come. Gaston had dreaded this hour, though he knew it would come one day. A woman on a death-bed has a right to ask for and get the truth. He had forborne telling her of her son; and she, whenever she had seen him, had contented herself with asking general questions, dreading in her heart that Jock had died a dreadful or shameful death, or else this gentleman would, voluntarily, say more. But, herself on her way out of the world, as she feared, wished the truth, whatever it might be.

Gaston told Cawley that he would drive over at once, and then asked who it was had called out at him. A drunken, poaching fellow, he was told, who in all the years since Jock had gone, had never passed the inn without stopping to say: "Where's my old chum, Jock Lawson?" In the past he and Jock had been in more than one scrape together. He had learned from Mrs. Cawley that Gaston had known Jock in Canada.

When Cawley had gone, Gaston turned to the other gentlemen present.

"An original speech, upon my word, Belward," said Captain Maudsley.

Mr. Warren Gasgoyne came.

"You are expected to lunch or something to-morrow, Belward, you remember? Devil of a speech that! But, if you will 'allow me to speak, me noble lord,' you are the rankest Conservative of us all."

"Don't you know that the easiest constitutional step is from a republic to an autocracy, and vice versa?"

"I don't know it, and I don't know how you do it."

"Do what?"

"Make them think as you do."

He waved his hand to the departing crowd.

"I don't. I try to think as they do. I am always in touch with the primitive mind."

"You ought to do great things here, Belward," said the other seriously. "You have the trick; and we need wisdom at Westminster."

"Don't be mistaken; I am only adaptable. There's frank confession."

At this point Mr. Babbs came up and said good-night in a large, self-conscious way. Gaston hoped that his campaign would not be wasted, and the fluffy gentleman retired. When he got out of earshot in the shadows, he turned and shook his fist towards Gaston, saying: "Half-breed upstart!" Then he refreshed his spirits by swearing at his coachman.

Gaston and Jacques drove quickly over to "The Whisk o' Barley." Gaston was now intent to tell the whole truth. He wished that he had done it before; but his motives had been good—it was not to save himself. Yet he shrank. Presently he thought:

"What is the matter with me? Before I came here, if I had an idea I stuck to it, and didn't have any nonsense when I knew I was right. I am getting sensitive—the thing I find everywhere in this country: fear of feeling or giving pain, as though the bad tooth out isn't better than the bad tooth in. When I really get sentimental I'll fold my Arab tent—so help me, ye seventy Gods of Yath!"

A little while after he was at Mrs. Cawley's bed, the landlord handing him a glass of hot grog, Jock's mother eyeing him feverishly from the quilt. Gaston quietly felt her wrist, counting the pulse-beats; then told Cawley to wet a cloth and hand it to him. He put it gently on the woman's head. The eyes of the woman followed him anxiously. He sat down again, and in response to her questioning gaze, began the story of Jock's life as he knew it.

Cawley stood leaning on the foot-board; the woman's face was cowled in the quilt with hungry eyes; and Gaston's voice went on in a low monotone, to the ticking of the great clock in the next room. Gaston watched her face, and there came to him like an inspiration little things Jock did, which would mean more to his mother than large adventures. Her lips moved now and again, even a smile flickered. At last Gaston came to his father's own death and the years that followed; then the events in Labrador.

He approached this with unusual delicacy: it needed bravery to look into the mother's eyes, and tell the story. He did not know how dramatically he told it—how he etched it without a waste word. When he came to that scene in the Fort, the three men sitting, targets for his bullets,—he softened the details greatly. He did not tell it as he told it at the Court, but the simpler, sparser language made it tragically clear. There was no sound from the bed, none from the foot-board, but he heard a door open and shut without, and footsteps somewhere near.

How he put the body in the tree, and prayed over it and left it there, was all told; and then he paused. He turned a little sick as he saw the white face before him. She drew herself up, her fingers caught away the night-dress at her throat; she stared hard at him for a moment, and then, with a wild, moaning voice, cried out:

"You killed my boy! You killed my boy! You killed my boy!"

Gaston was about to take her hand, when he heard a shuffle and a rush behind him. He rose, turned swiftly, saw a bottle swinging, threw up his hand . . . and fell backwards against the bed.

The woman caught his bleeding head to her breast and hugged it.

"My Jock, my poor boy!" she cried in delirium now. Cawley had thrown his arms about the struggling, drunken assailant—Jock's poaching friend.

The mother now called out to the pinioned man, as she had done to Gaston:

"You have killed my boy!" She kissed Gaston's bloody face.

A messenger was soon on the way to Ridley Court, and in a little upper room Jacques was caring for his master.

CHAPTER IX

HE FINDS NEW SPONSORS

Gaston lay for many days at "The Whisk o' Barley." During that time the inn was not open to customers. The woman also for two days hung at the point of death, and then rallied. She remembered the events of the painful night, and often asked after Gaston. Somehow, her horror of her son's death at his hands was met by the injury done him now. She vaguely felt that there had been justice and punishment. She knew that in the room at Labrador Gaston Belward had been scarcely less mad than her son.

Gaston, as soon as he became conscious, said that his assailant must be got out of the way of the police, and to that end bade Jacques send for Mr. Warren Gasgoyne. Mr. Gasgoyne and Sir William arrived at the same time, but Gaston was unconscious again. Jacques, however, told them what his master's wishes were, and they were carried out; Jock's friend secretly left England forever. Sir William and Mr. Gasgoyne got the whole tale from the landlord, whom they asked to say nothing publicly.

Lady Belward drove down each day, and sat beside him for a couple of hours-silent, solicitous, smoothing his pillow or his wasting hand. The brain had been injured, and recovery could not be immediate. Hovey the housekeeper had so begged to be installed as nurse, that her wish was granted, and she was with him night and day. Now she shook her head at him sadly, now talked in broken sentences to herself, now bustled about silently, a tyrant to the other servants sent down from the Court. Every day also the headgroom and the huntsman came, and in the village Gaston's humble friends discussed the mystery, stoutly defending him when some one said it was "more nor gabble, that theer saying o' the poacher at the meetin.'"

But the landlord and his wife kept silence, the officers of the law took no action, and the town and country newspapers could do no more than speak of "A vicious assault upon the heir of Ridley Court." It had become the custom now to leave Ian out of that question. But the wonder died as all wonders do, and Gaston made his fight for health.

The day before he was removed to the Court, Mrs. Cawley was helped upstairs to see him. She was gaunt and hollow-eyed. Lady Belward and Mrs. Gasgoyne were present. The woman made her respects, and then stood at Gaston's bedside. He looked up with a painful smile.

"Do you forgive me?" he asked. "I've almost paid!"

He touched his bandaged head.

"It ain't for mothers to forgi'e the thing," she replied, in a steady voice, "but I can forgi'e the man. 'Twere done i' madness—there beant the will workin' i' such. 'Twere a comfort that he'd a prayin' over un."

Gaston took the gnarled fingers in his. It had never struck him how dreadful a thing it was—so used had he been to death in many forms—till he had told the story to this mother.

"Mrs. Cawley," he said, "I can't make up to you what Jock would have been; but I can do for you in one way as much as Jock. This house is yours from to-day."

He drew a deed from the coverlet, and handed it to her. He had got it from Sir William that morning. The poor and the crude in mind can only understand an objective emotion, and the counters for these are this world's goods. Here was a balm in Gilead. The love of her child was real, but the consolation was so practical to Mrs. Cawley that the lips which might have cursed, said:

"Ah, sir, the wind do be fittin' the shore lamb! I' the last Judgen, I'll no speak agen 'ee. I be sore fretted harm come to 'ee."

At this Mrs. Gasgoyne rose, and in her bustling way dismissed the grateful peasant, who fondled the deed and called eagerly down the stairs to her husband as she went.

Mrs. Gasgoyne then came back, sat down, and said: "Now you needn't fret about that any longer—barbarian!" she added, shaking a finger. "Didn't I say that you would get into trouble? that you would set the country talking? Here you were, in the dead of night, telling ghost stories, and raking up your sins, with no cause whatever, instead of in your bed. You were to have lunched with us the next day—I had asked Lady Harriet to meet you, too!—and you didn't; and you have wretched patches where your hair ought to be. How can you promise that you'll not make a madder sensation some day?"

Gaston smiled up at her. Her fresh honesty, under the guise of banter, was always grateful to him. He shook his head, smiled, and said nothing.

She went on.

"I want a promise that you will do what your godfather and godmother will swear for you."

She acted on him like wine.

"Of course, anything. Who are my godfather and godmother?"

She looked him steadily, warmly in the eyes: "Warren and myself."

Now he understood: his promise to his grandmother and grandfather. So, they had spoken! He was sure that Mrs. Gasgoyne had objected. He knew that behind her playful treatment of the subject there was real scepticism of himself. It put him on his mettle, and yet he knew she read him deeper than any one else, and flattered him least.

He put out his hand, and took hers.

"You take large responsibilities," he said, "but I will try and justify you—honestly, yes."

In her hearty way, she kissed him on the cheek. "There," she responded, "if you and Delia do make up your minds, see that you treat her well. And you are to come, just as soon as you are able, to stay at Peppingham. Delia, silly child, is anxious, and can't see why she mustn't call with me now."

In his room at the Court that night, Gaston inquired of Jacques about Alice Wingfield, and was told that on the day of the accident she had left with her grandfather for the Continent. He was not sorry. For his own sake he could have wished an understanding between them. But now he was on the way to marriage, and it was as well that there should be no new situations. The girl could not wish the thing known. There would be left him, in this case, to befriend her should it ever be needed. He remembered the spring of pleasure he felt when he first saw other faces like his father's—his grandfather's, his grandmother's. But this girl's was so different to him; having the tragedy of the lawless, that unconscious suffering stamped by the mother upon the child. There was, however, nothing to be done. He must wait.

Two days later Lady Dargan called to inquire after him. He was lying in his study with a book, and Lady Belward sent to ask him if he would care to see her and Lord Dargan's nephew, Cluny Vosse. Lady Belward did not come; Sir William brought them. Lady Dargan came softly to him, smiled more with her eyes than her lips, and told him how sorry she had been to hear of his illness. Some months before Gaston had met Cluny Vosse, who at once was his admirer. Gaston liked the youth. He was fresh, high-minded, extravagant, idle; but he had no vices, and no particular vanity save for his personal appearance. His face was ever radiant with health, shining with satisfaction. People liked him, and did not discount it by saying that he had nothing in him. Gaston liked him most because he was so wholly himself, without guile, beautifully honest.

Now Cluny sat down, tapped the crown of his hat, looked at him cheerily, and said:

"Got in a cracker, didn't he?"

Gaston nodded, amused.

"The fellows at Brooke's had a talkee-talkee, and they'd twenty different stories. Of course it was rot. We were all cut up though and hoped you'd pull through. Of course there couldn't be any doubt of that— you've been through too many, eh?"

Cluny always assumed that Gaston had had numberless tragical adventures which, if told, must make Dumas turn in his grave with envy.

Gaston smiled, and laid a hand upon the other's knee. "I'm not shell-proof, Vosse, and it was rather a narrow squeak, I'm told. But I'm kept, you see, for a worse fate and a sadder."

"I say, Belward, you don't mean that! Your eyes go so queer sometimes, that a chap doesn't know what to think. You ought to live to a hundred. You'll have to. You've got it all—"

"Oh no, my boy, I haven't got anything." He waved his hand pleasantly towards his grandfather. "I'm on the knees of the gods merely."

Cluny turned on Sir William.

"It isn't any secret, is it, sir? He gets the lot, doesn't he?"

Sir William's occasional smile came.

"I fancy there's some condition about the plate, the pictures, and the title; but I do not suppose that matters meanwhile."

He spoke half-musingly and with a little unconscious irony, and the boy, vaguely knowing that there was a cross-current somewhere, drifted.

"No, of course not; he can have fun enough without them, can't he?"

Lady Dargan here soothingly broke in, inquiring about Gaston's illness, and showing a tactful concern. But the nephew persisted:

"I say, Belward, Aunt Sophie was cut up no end when she heard of it. She wouldn't go out to dinner that night at Lord Dunfolly's, and, of course, I didn't go. And I wanted to; for Delia Gasgoyne was to be there, and she's ripping."

Lady Dargan, in spite of herself, blushed, but without confusion, and Gaston adroitly led the conversation otherwhere. Presently she said that they were to be at their villa in France during the late summer, and if he chanced to be abroad would he come? He said that he intended to visit his uncle in Paris, but that afterwards he would be glad to visit them for a short time.

She looked astonished. "With your uncle Ian!"

"Yes. He is to show me art-life, and all that."

She looked troubled. He saw that she wished to say something.

"Yes, Lady Dargan?" he asked.

She spoke with fluttering seriousness.

"I asked you once to come to me if you ever needed a friend. I do not wait for that. I ask you not to go to your uncle."

"Why?"

He was thinking that, despite social artifice and worldliness, she was sentimental.

"Because there will be trouble. I can see it. You may trust a woman's instinct; and I know that man!" He did not reply at once, but presently said:

"I fancy I must keep my promise."

"What is the book you are reading?" she said, changing the subject, for Sir William was listening.

He opened it, and smiled musingly.

"It is called Affairs of Some Consequence in the Reign of Charles I. In reading it I seemed to feel that it was incorrect, and my mind kept wandering away into patches of things—incidents, scenes, bits of talk —as I fancied they really were, not apocryphal or 'edited' as here."

"I say," said Cluny, "that's rum, isn't it?"

"For instance," Gaston continued, "this tale of King Charles and Buckingham." He read it. "Now here is the scene as I picture it." In quick elliptical phrases he gave the tale from a different stand-point.

Sir William stared curiously at Gaston, then felt for some keys in his pocket. He got up and rang the bell. Gaston was still talking. He gave the keys to Falby with a whispered word. In a few moments Falby placed a small leather box beside Sir William, and retired at a nod. Sir William presently said: "Where did you read those things?"

"I do not know that I ever read them."

"Did your father tell you them?"

"I do not remember so, though he may have."

"Did you ever see this box?"

"Never before."

"You do not know what is in it?"

"Not in the least."

"And you have never seen this key?"

"Not to my knowledge."

"It is very strange." He opened the box. "Now, here are private papers of Sir Gaston Belward, more than two hundred years old, found almost fifty years ago by myself in the office of our family solicitor. Listen."

He then began to read from the faded manuscript. A mysterious feeling pervaded the room. Once or twice Cluny gave a dry nervous kind of laugh. Much of what Gaston had said was here in stately old-fashioned language. At a certain point the MS. ran:

"I drew back and said, 'As your grace will have it, then—'"

Here Gaston came to a sitting posture, and interrupted.

"Wait, wait!"

He rose, caught one of two swords that were crossed on the wall, and stood out.

"This is how it was. 'As your grace will have it, then, to no waste of time!' We fell to. First he came carefully and made strange feints, learned at King Louis's Court, to try my temper. But I had had these tricks of my cousin Secord, and I returned his sport upon him. Then he came swiftly, and forced me back upon the garden wall. I gave to him foot by foot, for he was uncommon swift and dexterous. He pinched me sorely once under the knee, and I returned him one upon the wrist, which sent a devilish fire into his eyes. At that his play became so delicate and confusing that I felt I should go dizzy if it stayed; so I tried the one great trick cousin Secord taught me, making to run him through, as a last effort. The thing went wrong, but checking off my blunder he blundered too,—out of sheer wonder, perhaps, at my bungling,—and I disarmed him. So droll was it that I laughed outright, and he, as quick in humour as in temper, stood hand on hip, and presently came to a smile. With that my cousin Secord cried: 'The king! the king!' I got me up quickly—"

Here Gaston, who had in a kind of dream acted the whole scene, swayed with faintness, and Cluny caught him, saving him from a fall. Cluny's colour was all gone. Lady Dargan had sat dazed, and Sir William's face was anxious, puzzled.

A few hours later Sir William was alone with Gaston, who was recovered and cool.

"Gaston," he said, "I really do not understand this faculty of memory, or whatever it is. Have you any idea how you come by it?"

"Have we any idea how life comes and goes, sir?"

"I confess not. I confess not, really."

"Well, I'm in the dark about it too; but I sometimes fancy that I'm mixed up with that other Gaston."

"It sounds fantastic."

"It is fantastic. Now, here is this manuscript, and here is a letter I wrote this morning. Put them together."

Sir William did so.

"The handwriting is singularly like."

"Well," continued Gaston, smiling whimsically, "suppose that I am Sir Gaston Belward, Baronet, who is thought to lie in the church yonder, the title is mine, isn't it?"

Sir William smiled also.

"The evidence is scarce enough to establish succession."

"But there would be no succession. A previous holder of the title isn't dead: ergo, the present holder, has no right."

Gaston had shaded his eyes with his hand, and he was watching Sir William's face closely, out of curiosity chiefly. Sir William regarded the thing with hesitating humour.

"Well, well, suppose so. The property was in the hands of a younger branch of the family then. There was no entail, as now."

"Wasn't there?" said Gaston enigmatically.

He was thinking of some phrases in a manuscript which he had found in this box.

"Perhaps where these papers came from there are others," he added.

Sir William lifted his eyebrows ironically. "I hardly think so."

Gaston laughed, not wishing him to take the thing at all seriously. He continued airily:

"It would be amusing if the property went with the title after all, wouldn't it, sir?"

Sir William got to his feet and said testily: "That should never be while I lived."

"Of course not, sir."

Sir William saw the bull, and laughed, heartily for him.

They bade each other good-night.

"I'll have a look in the solicitor's office all the same," said Gaston to himself.

CHAPTER X

HE COMES TO "THE WAKING OF THE FIRE"

A few days afterwards Gaston joined a small party at Peppingham. Without any accent life was made easy for him. He was alone much, and yet, to himself, he seemed to have enough of company.

The situation did not impose itself conspicuously. Delia gave him no especial reason to be vain. She had not an exceeding wit, but she had charm, and her talk was interesting to Gaston, who had come, for the first time, into somewhat intimate relations with an English girl. He was struck with her conventional delicacy and honour on one side, and the limitation of her ideas on the other. But with it all she had some slight touch of temperament which lifted her from the usual level. And just now her sprightliness was more marked than it had ever been.

Her great hour seemed come to her. She knew that there had been talk among the elders, and what was meant by Gaston's visit. Still, they were not much alone together. Gaston saw her mostly with others. Even a woman with a tender strain for a man knows what will serve for her ascendancy: the graciousness of her disposition, the occasional flash of her mother's temper, and her sense of being superior to a situation—the gift of every well-bred English girl.

Cluny Vosse was also at the house, and his devotion was divided between Delia and Gaston. Cluny was a great favourite, and Agatha Gasgoyne, who had a wild sense of humour, egged him on with her sister, which gave Delia enough to do. At last Cluny, in a burst of confidence, declared that he meant to propose to Delia. Agatha then became serious, and said that Delia was at least four years older than himself, that he was just her—Agatha's—age, and that the other match would be very unsuitable. This put Cluny on Delia's defence, and he praised her youth, and hinted at his own elderliness. He had lived, he had seen It (Cluny called the world and all therein "It"), he was aged; he was in the large eye of experience; he had outlived the vices and the virtues of his time, which, told in his own naive staccato phrases, made Agatha hug herself. She advised him to go and ask Mr. Belward's advice; begged him not to act until he had done so. And Cluny, who was blind as a bat when a woman mocked him, went to Gaston and said:

"See, old chap,—I know you don't mind my calling you that—I've come for advice. Agatha said I'd better. A fellow comes to a time when he says, 'Here, I want a shop of my own,' doesn't he? He's seen It, he's had It all colours, he's ready for family duties, and the rest. That's so, isn't it?"

Gaston choked back a laugh, and, purposely putting himself on the wrong scent, said:

"And does Agatha agree?"

"Agatha? Come, Belward, that youngster! Agatha's only in on a sisterly-brotherly basis. Now, see I've got a little load of L s. d., and I'm to get more, especially if Uncle Dick keeps on thinking I am artless. Well, why shouldn't I marry?"

"No reason against it, if husband and father in you yearn for bibs and petticoats."

"I say, Belward, don't laugh!"

"I never was more serious. Who is the girl?"

"She looks up to you as I do-of course that's natural; and if it comes off, no one'll have a jollier corner chez nous. It's Delia."

"Delia? Delia who?"

"Why, Delia Gasgoyne. I haven't done the thing quite regular, I know. I ought to have gone to her people first; but they know all about me, and so does Delia, and I'm on the spot, and it wouldn't look well to be taking advantage of that with her father and mother-they'd feel bound to be hospitable. So I've just gone on my own tack, and I've come to Agatha and you. Agatha said to ask you if I'd better speak to Delia now."

"My dear Cluny, are you very much in love?"

"That sounds religious, doesn't it—a kind of Nonconformist business? I think she's the very finest. A fellow'd hold himself up, 'd be a deuce of a swell—and, hang it all, I hate breakfasting alone!"

"Yes, yes, Cluny; but what about a pew in church, with regular attendance, and a justice of the peace, and little Cluny Vosses on the carpet?"

Cluny's face went crimson.

"I say, Belward, I've seen It all, of course; I know It backwards, and I'm not squeamish, but that sounds—flippant-that, with her."

Gaston reached out and caught the boy's shoulder. "Don't do it, Cluny. Spare yourself. It couldn't come off. Agatha knows that, I fancy. She is a little sportsman. I might let you go and speak; but I think my chances are better than yours, Cluny. Hadn't you better let me try first? Then, if I fail, your chances are still the same, eh?"

Cluny gasped. His warm face went pale, then shot to purple, and finally settled into a grey ruddiness. "Belward," he said at last, "I didn't know; upon my soul, I didn't know, or I'd have cut off my head first."

"My dear Cluny, you shall have your chance; but let me go first, I'm older."

"Belward, don't take me for a fool. Why, my trying what you go to do is like—is like—"

Cluny's similes failed to come.

"Like a fox and a deer on the same trail?"

"I don't understand that. Like a yeomanry steeplechase to Sandown—is that it? Belward, I'm sorry. Playing it so low on a chap you like!"

"Don't say a word, Cluny; and, believe me, you haven't yet seen all of It. There's plenty of time. When you really have had It, you will learn to say of a woman, not that she's the very finest, and that you hate breakfasting alone, but something that'll turn your hair white, or keep you looking forty when you're sixty."

That evening Gaston dressed with unusual care. When he entered the drawing-room, he looked as handsome as a man need in this world. His illness had refined his features and form, and touched off his cheerfulness with a fine melancholy. Delia glowed as she saw the admiring glances sent his way, but burned with anger when she also saw that he was to take in Lady Gravesend to dinner; for Lady Gravesend had spoken slightingly of Gaston—had, indeed, referred to his "nigger blood!" And now her mother had sent her in to dinner on his arm, she affable, too affable by a great deal. Had she heard the dry and subtle suggestion of Gaston's talk, she would, however, have justified her mother.

About half past nine Delia was in the doorway, talking to one of the guests, who, at the call of some one else, suddenly left her. She heard a voice behind her. "Will you not sing?"

She thrilled, and turned to say: "What shall I sing, Mr. Belward?"

"The song I taught you the other day—'The Waking of the Fire.'"

"But I've never sung it before anybody."

"Do I not count?—But, there, that's unfair! Believe me, you sing it very well."

She lifted her eyes to his:

"You do not pay compliments, and I believe you. Your 'very well' means much. If you say so, I will do my best."

"I say so. You are amenable. Is that your mood to-night?" He smiled brightly.

Her eyes flashed with a sweet malice.

"I am not at all sure. It depends on how your command to sing is justified."

"You cannot help but sing well."

"Why?"

"Because I will help you—make you."

This startled her ever so little. Was there some fibre of cruelty in him, some evil in this influence he had over her? She shrank, and yet again she said that she would rather have his cruelty than another man's tenderness, so long as she knew that she had his— She paused, and did not say the word. She met his eyes steadily—their concentration dazed her—then she said almost coldly, her voice sounding far away:

"How, make me?"

"How fine, how proud!" he said to himself, then added:

"I meant 'make' in the helpful sense. I know the song: I've heard it sung, I've sung it; I've taught you; my mind will act on yours, and you will sing it well."

"Won't you sing it yourself? Do, please."

"No; to-night I wish to hear you."

"Why?"

"I will tell you later. Can you play the accompaniment? If not, I—"

"Oh, will you? I could sing it then, I think. You played it so beautifully the other day—with all those strange chords."

He smiled.

"It is one of the few things that I can play. I always had a taste for music; and up in one of the forts there was an old melodeon, so I hammered away for years. I had to learn difficult things at the start, or none at all, or else those I improvised; and that's how I can play one or two of Beethoven's symphonies pretty well, and this song, and a few others, and go a cropper with a waltz. Will you come?"

They moved to the piano. No one at first noticed them. When he sat down, he said:

"You remember the words?"

"Yes, I learned them by heart."

"Good!"

He gently struck the chords. His gentleness had, however, a firmness, a deep persuasiveness, which drew every face like a call. A few chords waving, as it were, over the piano, and then he whispered:

"Now."

"Please go on for a minute longer," she begged.

"My throat feels dry all at once."

"Face away from the rest, towards me," he said gently.

She did so. His voice took a note softly, and held it. Presently her voice as softly joined it, his stopped, and hers went on:

> "In the lodge of the Mother of Men,
> In the land of Desire,
> Are the embers of fire,
> Are the ashes of those who return,
> Who return to the world:
> Who flame at the breath
> Of the Mockers of Death.
> O Sweet, we will voyage again
> To the camp of Love's fire,
>   Nevermore to return!"

"How am I doing?" she said at the end of this verse. She really did not know—her voice seemed an endless distance away. But she felt the stillness in the drawing-room.

"Well," he said. "Now for the other. Don't be afraid; let your voice, let yourself, go."

"I can't let myself go."

"Yes, you can: just swim with the music."

She did swim with it. Never before had Peppingham drawing-room heard a song like this; never before, never after, did any of Delia Gasgoyne's friends hear her sing as she did that night. And Lady Gravesend whispered for a week afterwards that Delia Gasgoyne sang a wild love song in the most abandoned way with that colonial Belward. Really a song of the most violent sentiment!

There had been witchery in it all. For Gaston lifted the girl on the waves of his music, and did what he pleased with her, as she sang:

> "O love, by the light of thine eye
> We will fare oversea,
> We will be

> As the silver-winged herons that rest
> By the shallows,
> The shallows of sapphire stone;
> No more shall we wander alone.
> As the foam to the shore
> Is my spirit to thine;
> And God's serfs as they fly,—
> The Mockers of Death
> They will breathe on the embers of fire:
> We shall live by that breath,—
> Sweet, thy heart to my heart,
> As we journey afar,
> No more, nevermore, to return!"

When the song was ended there was silence, then an eager murmur, and requests for more; but Gaston, still lengthening the close of the accompaniment, said quietly:

"No more. I wanted to hear you sing that song only."

He rose.

"I am so very hot," she said.

"Come into the hall."

They passed into the long corridor, and walked up and down, for a time in silence.

"You felt that music?" he asked at last.

"As I never felt music before," she replied.

"Do you know why I asked you to sing it?"

"How should I know?"

"To see how far you could go with it."

"How far did I go?"

"As far as I expected."

"It was satisfactory?"

"Perfectly."

"But why—experiment—on me?"

"That I might see if you were not, after all, as much a barbarian as I."

"Am I?"

"No. That was myself singing as well as you. You did not enjoy it altogether, did you?"

"In a way, yes. But—shall I be honest? I felt, too, as if, somehow, it wasn't quite right; so much—what shall I call it?"

"So much of old Adam and the Garden? Sit down here for a moment, will you?"

She trembled a little, and sat.

"I want to speak plainly and honestly to you," he said, looking earnestly at her. "You know my history—about my wife who died in Labrador, and all the rest?"

"Yes, they have told me."

"Well, I have nothing to hide, I think; nothing more that you ought to know: though I've been a scamp one way and another."

"'That I ought to know'?" she repeated.

"Yes: for when a man asks a woman to be his wife, he should be prepared to open the cupboard of skeletons." She was silent; her heart was beating so hard that it hurt her.

"I am going to ask you to be my wife, Delia."

She was silent, and sat motionless, her hands clasped in her lap.

He went on

"I don't know that you will be wise to accept me, but if you will take the risk—"

"Oh, Gaston, Gaston!" she said, and her hands fluttered towards his.

An hour later, he said to her, as they parted for the night:

"I hope, with all my heart, that you will never repent of it, Delia."

"You can make me not repent of it. It rests with you, Gaston; indeed, indeed, all with you."

"Poor girl!" he said, unconsciously, as he entered his room. He could not have told why he said it. "Why will you always sit up for me, Brillon?" he asked a moment afterwards.

Jacques saw that something had occurred. "I have nothing else to do, sir," he replied. 'Brillon," Gaston added presently, "we're in a devil of a scrape now."

"What shall we do, monsieur?"

"Did we ever turn tail?"

"Yes, from a prairie fire."

"Not always. I've ridden through."

"Alors, it's one chance in ten thousand!"

"There's a woman to be thought of—Jacques."

"There was that other time."

"Well, then?"

Presently Jacques said: "Who is she, monsieur?"

Gaston did not answer. He was thinking hard. Jacques said no more. The next morning early the guests knew who the woman was, and by noon Jacques also.

CHAPTER XI

HE MAKES A GALLANT CONQUEST

Gaston let himself drift. The game of love and marriage is exciting, the girl was affectionate and admiring, the world was genial, and all things came his way. Towards the end of the hunting season Captain Maudsley had an accident. It would prevent him riding to hounds again, and at his suggestion, backed by Lord Dunfolly and Lord Dargan, Gaston became Master of the Hounds. His grandfather and great-grandfather had been Master of the Hounds before him. Hunting was a keen enjoyment—one outlet for wild life in him—and at the last meet of the year he rode in Captain Maudsley's place. They had a good run, and the taste of it remained with Gaston for many a day; he thought of it sometimes as he rode in the Park now every morning—with Delia and her mother.

Jacques and his broncho came no more, or if they did it was at unseasonable hours, and then to be often reprimanded (and twice arrested) for furious riding. Gaston had a bad moment when he told Jacques that he need not come with him again. He did it casually, but, cool as he was, a cold sweat came on his cheek. He had to take a little brandy to steady himself—yet he had looked into menacing rifle-barrels more than once without a tremor. It was clear, on the face of it, that Delia and her mother should be his companions in the Park, and not this grave little half-breed; but, somehow, it got on his nerves. He hesitated for days before he could cast the die against Jacques. It had been the one open bond of the old life; yet the man was but a servant, and to be treated as such, and was, indeed, except on rarest occasions. If Delia had known that Gaston balanced the matter between her and Jacques, her indignation might perhaps have sent matters to a crisis. But Gaston did the only possible thing; and the weeks drifted on.

Happy? It was inexplicable even to himself that at times, when he left Delia, he said unconsciously: "Well, it's a pity!"

But she was happy in her way. His dark, mysterious face with its background of abstraction, his unusual life, distinguished presence, and the fact that people of great note sought his conversation, all strengthened the bonds, and deepened her imagination; and imagination is at the root of much that passes for love. Gaston was approached at Lord Dargan's house by the Premier himself. It was suggested that he should stand for a constituency in the Conservative interest. Lord Faramond, himself picturesque, acute, with a keen knowledge of character and a taste for originality, saw material for a useful supporter—fearless, independent, with a gift for saying ironical things, and some primitive and fundamental principles well digested.

Gaston, smiling, said that he would only be a buffalo fretting on a chain.

Lord Faramond replied:

"And why the chain?" He followed this up by saying: "It is but a case of playing lion-tamer down there. Have one little gift all your own, know when to impose it, and you have the pleasure of feeling that your fingers move a great machine, the greatest in the world—yes the very greatest. There is Little Grapnel just vacant: the faithful Glynn is gone. Come: if you will, I'll send my secretary to-morrow morning-eh?"

"You are not afraid of the buffalo, sir?"

Lord Faramond's fingers touched his arm, drummed it "My greatest need— one to roar as gently as the sucking-dove."

"But what if I, not knowing the rules of the game, should think myself on the corner of the veldt or in an Indian's tepee, and hit out?"

"You do not carry derringers?"

He smiled. "No; but—"

He glanced down at his arms.

"Well, well; that will come one day, perhaps!" Lord Faramond paused, abstracted, then added: "But not through you. Good-bye, then, good-bye. Little Grapnel in ten days!"

And it was so. Little Grapnel was Conservative. It was mostly a matter of nomination, and in two weeks Gaston, in a kind of dream, went down to Westminster, lunched with Lord Faramond, and was introduced to the House. The Ladies Gallery was full, for the matter was in all the papers, and a pretty sensation had been worked up one way and another.

That night, after dinner, Gaston rose to make his maiden speech on a bill dealing with an imminent social question. He was not an amateur. Time upon time he had addressed gatherings in the North, and had once stood at the bar of the Canadian Commons to plead the cause of the half-breeds. He was pale, but firm, and looked striking. His eyes went slowly round the House, and he began in a low, clear, deliberate voice, which got attention at once. The first sentence was, however, a surprise to every one, and not the least to his own party, excepting Lord Faramond. He disclaimed detailed and accurate knowledge of the subject. He said this with an honesty which took away the breath of the House. In a quiet, easy tone he then referred to what had been previously said in the debate.

The first thing he did was to crumble away with a regretful kind of superiority the arguments of two Conservative speakers, to the sudden amusement of the Opposition, who presently cheered him. He looked up as though a little surprised, waited patiently, and went on. The iconoclasm proceeded. He had one or two fixed ideas in his mind, simple principles on social questions of which he had spoken to his leader, and he never wavered from the sight of them, though he had yet to state them. The Premier sat, head cocked, with an ironical smile at the cheering, but he was wondering whether, after all, his man was sure; whether he could stand this fire, and reverse his engine quite as he intended. One of the previous speakers was furious, came over and appealed to Lord Faramond, who merely said, "Wait."

Gaston kept on. The flippant amusement of the Opposition continued. Something, however, in his grim steadiness began to impress his own party as the other, while from more than one quarter of the House there came a murmur of sympathy. His courage, his stone-cold strength, the disdain which was coming into his voice, impressed them, apart from his argument or its bearing on the previous debate. Lord Faramond heard the occasional murmurs of approval and smiled. Then there came a striking silence, for Gaston paused. He looked towards the Ladies Gallery. As if in a dream—for his brain was working with clear, painful power—he saw, not Delia nor her mother, nor Lady Dargan, but Alice Wingfield! He had a sting, a rush in his blood. He felt that none had an interest in him such as she: shamed, sorrowful, denied the compensating comfort which his brother's love might give her. Her face, looking through the barriers, pale, glowing, anxious, almost weird, seemed set to the bars of a cage.

Gaston turned upon the House, and flashed a glance towards Lord Faramond, who, turned round on the Treasury Bench, was looking up at him. He began slowly to pit against his former startling admissions the testimony of his few principles, and to buttress them on every side with apposite observations, naive, pungent. Presently there came a poignant edge to his trailing tones. After giving the subject new points of view, showing him to have studied Whitechapel as well as Kicking Horse Pass, he contended that no social problem could be solved by a bill so crudely radical, so impractical.

He was saying: "In the history of the British Parliament—" when some angry member cried out, "Who coached you?"

Gaston's quick eye found the man.

"Once," he answered instantly, "one honourable gentleman asked that of another in King Charles's Parliament, and the reply then is mine now— 'You, sir!'"

"How?" returned the puzzled member.

Gaston smiled:

"The nakedness of the honourable gentleman's mind!"

The game was in his hands. Lord Faramond twisted a shoulder with satisfaction, tossed a whimsical look down the line of the Treasury Bench, and from that Bench came unusual applause.

"Where the devil did he get it?" queried a Minister.

"Out on the buffalo-trail," replied Lord Faramond. "Good fellow!"

In the Ladies Gallery, Delia clasped her mother's hand with delight; in the Strangers Gallery, a man said softly, "Not so bad, Cadet."

Alice Wingfield's face had a light of aching pleasure. "Gaston, Gaston!" she said, in a whisper heard only by the woman sitting next to her, who though a stranger gave a murmur of sympathy.

Gaston made his last effort in a comparison of the state of the English people now and before she became Cromwell's Commonwealth, and then incisively traced the social development onwards. It was the work of a man with a dramatic nature and a mathematical turn. He put the time, the manners, the movements, the men, as in a picture.

Presently he grew scornful. His words came hotly, like whip-lashes. He rose to force and power, though his voice was never loud, rather concentrated, resonant. It dropped suddenly to a tone of persuasiveness and conciliation, and declaring that the bill would be merely vicious where it meant to be virtuous, ended with the question:

"Shall we burn the house to roast the pig?"

"That sounds American," said the member for Burton-Halsey, "but he hasn't an accent. Pig is vulgar though—vulgar."

"Make it Lamb—make it Lamb!" urged his neighbour.

Meanwhile both sides applauded. Maiden speeches like this were not common. Lord Faramond turned round to him. Another member made way and Gaston leaned towards the Premier, who nodded and smiled. "Most excellent buffalo!" he said.

"One day we will chain you—to the Treasury Bench."

Gaston smiled.

"You are thought prudent, sir!"

"Ah! an enemy hath said this."

Gaston looked towards the Ladies Gallery. Delia's eyes were on him; Alice was gone.

A half-hour later he stood in the lobby, waiting for Mrs. Gasgoyne, Lady Dargan, and Delia to come. He had had congratulations in the House; he was having them now. Presently some one touched him on the arm.

"Not so bad, Cadet."

Gaston turned and saw his uncle. They shook hands. "You've a gift that way," Ian Belward continued, "but to what good? Bless you, the pot on the crackling thorns! Don't you find it all pretty hollow?"

Gaston was feeling reaction from the nervous work. "It is exciting."

"Yes, but you'll never have it again as to-night. The place reeks with smugness, vanity, and drudgery. It's only the swells—Derby, Gladstone, and the few—who get any real sport out of it. I can show you much more amusing things."

"For instance?"

"'Hast thou forgotten me?' You hungered for Paris and Art and the joyous life. Well, I'm ready. I want you. Paris, too, is waiting, and a good cuisine in a cheery menage. Sup with me at the Garrick, and I'll tell you. Come along. Quis separabit?"

"I have to wait for Mrs. Gasgoyne—and Delia."

"Delia! Delia! Goddess of proprieties, has it come to that!"

He saw a sudden glitter in Gaston's eyes, and changed his tone.

"Well, an' a man will he will, and he must be wished good-luck. So, good-luck to you! I'm sorry, though, for that cuisine in Paris, and the grand picnic at Fontainebleau, and Moban and Cerise. But it can't be helped."

He eyed Gaston curiously. Gaston was not in the least deceived. His uncle added presently, "But you will have supper with me just the same?"

Gaston consented, and at this point the ladies appeared. He had a thrill of pleasure at hearing their praises, but, somehow, of all the fresh experiences he had had in England, this, the weightiest, left him least elated. He had now had it all: the reaction was begun, and he knew it.

"Well, Ian Belward, what mischief are you at now?" said Mrs. Gasgoyne.

"A picture merely, and to offer homage. How have you tamed our lion, and how sweetly does he roar! I feed him at my Club to-night."

"Ian Belward, you are never so wicked as when you ought most to be decent—I wish I knew your place in this picture," she added brusquely.

"Merely a little corner at their fireside." He nodded towards Delia and Gaston.

"The man has sense, and Delia is my daughter!"

"Precisely why I wish a place in their affections."

"Why don't you marry one of the women you have—spoiled, and spend the rest of your time in living yourself down? You are getting old."

"For their own sakes, I don't. Put that to my credit. I'll have but one mistress only as the sand gets low. I've been true to her."

"You, true to anything!"

"The world has said so."

"Nonsense! You couldn't be."

"Visit my new picture in three months—my biggest thing. You will say my mistress fares well at my hands."

"Mere talk. I have seen your mistress, and before every picture I have thought of those women! A thing cannot be good at your price: so don't talk that sentimental stuff to me."

"Be original; you said that to me thirty years ago."

"I remember perfectly: that did not require much sense."

"No; you tossed it off, as it were. Yet I'd have made you a good husband. You are the most interesting woman I've ever met."

"The compliment is not remarkable. Now, Ian Belward, don't try to say clever things. And remember that I will have no mischief-making."

"At thy command—"

"Oh, cease acting, and take Sophie to her carriage." Two hours later, Delia Gasgoyne sat in her bedroom wondering at Gaston's abstraction during the drive home. Yet she had a proud elation at his success, and a happy tear came to her eye.

Meanwhile Gaston was supping with his uncle. Ian was in excellent spirits: brilliant, caustic, genial, suggestive. After a little while Gaston rose to the temper of his host. Already the scene in the Commons was fading from him, and when Ian proposed Paris immediately, he did not demur. The season was nearly over,

Ian said; very well, why remain? His attendance at the House? Well, it would soon be up for the session. Besides, the most effective thing he could do was to disappear for the time. Be unexpected—that was the key to notoriety.

Delia Gasgoyne? Well, as Gaston had said, they were to meet in the Mediterranean in September; meanwhile a brief separation would be good for both. Last of all—he did not wish to press it—but there was a promise!

Gaston answered quietly, at last: "I will redeem the promise."

"When?"

"Within thirty-six hours."

"That is, you will be at my studio in Paris within thirty-six hours from now?"

"That is it."

"Good! I shall start at eight to-morrow morning. You will bring your horse, Cadet?"

"Yes, and Brillon."

"He isn't necessary." Ian's brow clouded slightly.

"Absolutely necessary."

"A fantastic little beggar. You can get a better valet in France. Why have one at all?"

"I shall not decline from Brillon on a Parisian valet. Besides, he comes as my camarade."

"Goth! Goth! My friend the valet! Cadet, you're a wonderful fellow, but you'll never fit in quite."

"I don't wish to fit in; things must fit me." Ian smiled to himself.

"He has tasted it all—it's not quite satisfying—revolution next! What a smash-up there'll be! The romantic, the barbaric overlaps. Well, I shall get my picture out of it, and the estate too."

Gaston toyed with his wine-glass, and was deep in thought. Strange to say, he was seeing two pictures. The tomb of Sir Gaston in the little church at Ridley: A gipsy's van on the crest of a common, and a girl standing in the doorway.

Milton Keynes UK
Ingram Content Group UK Ltd.
UKHW040312181024
449757UK00005B/505